Prospecting
and
Setting Appointments
Made Easy

BARRY ANDRUSCHAK

ILLUSTRATIONS BY JOE KING

Agio
PUBLISHING HOUSE

Agio ✠
PUBLISHING HOUSE

151 Howe Street, Victoria BC Canada V8V 4K5

Prospecting and
Setting Appointments
Made Easy
ISBN 978-1-927755-16-7 (paperback)
ISBN 978-1-927755-17-4 (ebook)
Cataloguing information available from
Library and Archives Canada.

Printed on acid-free paper.

Agio Publishing House is a socially responsible company,
measuring success on a triple-bottom-line basis.

10 9 8 7 6 5 4 3 2 1b

Contents

Introduction

You can have the greatest idea, product or service to sell, but if you are unable to get people to listen to your presentation, chances are highly unlikely that you will succeed in making enough money to actually have a financially profitable business.

This book is for people who need to set appointments with other people to be successful in sales, relationships and life.

The tips contained here are mostly for beginning sales people to help them to properly approach and set appointments to make presentations to their "warm market" – essentially their family, friends, colleagues and acquaintances. This is not about cold calling or telemarketing, although the tips contained herein may help in those situations as well.

Experienced, seasoned veteran sales people who may be in a "sales slump" can also benefit by reviewing these basic and time-tested fundamentals. Sales managers will also benefit by giving their salespeople these tools to help them grow their clientele. This, in turn, will grow the manager's business.

This book is also for everyone and anyone who needs the co-operation of others at some point in their life and career. Getting people to listen to what you have to say is an important life skill. Once you learn these skills, you will have the keys to not only getting others to sit down and listen to you, but also how to teach these skills to others and empower them.

It'll even help you get dates. Yes. It'll help single men and women get dates. Because let's face it, isn't asking someone for a date, the same as asking for an appointment to make your best "pitch"? You are essentially selling your most valuable product – YOU. It is fundamentally the same when selling any product. You *must* first SELL YOURSELF.

How you approach the delicate art of asking for an appointment (or a date) may be the difference between success, frustration or failure in any arena of human interaction.

He or she who sets the most appointments will win over the long range. Why? Because having more appointments leads to more opportunities to give your presentation and ask for business. More closing opportunities leads to more sales and more income. You practice and polish your presentation and closing skills more often. You also develop a certain type of mental toughness that it takes to succeed in business because you experience more rejection, and learn how to minimize it and overcome it.

Rejection, like resistance in weight training, builds muscle – in this case, mental muscles.

One of the greatest rewards most winning sales people achieve is the mental toughness and positive mental attitude they develop. They believe they can accomplish anything … and consistently *do* achieve their goals. This, in turn, enables them to pass that belief on to others who are looking to them for leadership and guidance, especially their children.

My Story

From Zero to Hero

I started selling financial services (term insurance and mutual funds) in April of 1986 at age 26. By December of 1987, I was earning $10,000/month*. In today's dollars that would be $20,000/month. I started recruiting and training others to do the same thing and built a number of successful financial services businesses. I followed the same financial advice I gave my clients and associates and became financially free at age 30 with a residual income of over $100,000/year.

I took a couple years off, and then started again in a

---

* Of course, with this and all other incomes cited in this book, there is no guarantee other agents will achieve this level. The incomes one can achieve will vary widely according to skill, work ethic, ability and other factors.

city where I only knew 2 people and doubled my income to $200,000/year by 1993, and doubled it again by 1999. I semi-retired at age 42 and fully retired by age 50.

Despite this success, however, sales (prospecting, setting appointments and selling), was not my chosen career path.

I am a pilot by trade and an introvert by nature. I graduated with a diploma of Aviation Technology from Selkirk College in Castlegar, BC in 1982. Being that it was one of the best airline prep schools in the country, it was very expensive. But my parents and I thought it was worth it as it seemed virtually guaranteed I would be hired by a major airline right out of school.

Unfortunately, the country plunged into a big recession and the airlines were laying off hundreds of pilots. So I was forced to look for any fly-by-night charter airline that would hire me so I could build my time and pay off my student debts as well as survive. My first job was flying for a small company that paid me $500/month for about 10 hours of duty time a day. My rent was $250/month for a bachelor suite. I was so broke I could barely afford to put gas in my car or food in my belly.

My next few jobs were a little better, raising my pay to about $1,200 a month and allowing me to fly nicer aircraft. But again because the economy was so poor, I was laid off 5 times and fired twice in a span of 3 years.

I eventually landed a great job… (get it? Landed a job… pilots 'land' airplanes… Okay, never mind. That joke crashed and burned.)

Anyway, I landed a job flying charter in California and thought I had finally found my dream career path.

One day a pilot friend invited me to a seminar that really opened my eyes about how the financial services industry seemed to be taking advantage of consumers and our lack of financial education. I was very impressed with what this new company had to offer in terms of education and opportunity. They talked of writing my own paycheck, being my own boss, helping others to become financially independent. They said if I worked hard I could make $100,000 dollars a year by the time I was 30. I was 25 at the time, and also naive enough to believe that pitch. Much to my parents' extreme dismay and disappointment, I decided to leave my career as a pilot to begin a career as financial services sales person.

My dad warned me that the "pitch-men" were probably scamming me. The pitch that promised me I would be making $100,000 in 5 years was indeed incorrect. I made $100,000* in my second year. That sounds fast, but it was not easy. I worked 10 hours a day, 6 days a week mostly learning how to set appointments and sell, and then recruit and train others to do the same thing.

I learned by listening to others, and practicing, screwing up, practicing, screwing up and practicing some more. I hated the rejection, feared the phone, and wasn't outgoing enough to meet a lot of new people. But I wanted to succeed in the worst way.

So I took sales courses, read books, listened to older, experienced sales people. They all seemed super confident, and in my

---

* Again, a reminder that agents' incomes cannot be guaranteed. Actual incomes one will achieve vary widely according to skill, work ethic, ability, and other factors.

opinion, often super pushy. I was turned off by their techniques. I just didn't feel comfortable saying or using some of those techniques with friends and family. Their words and phrases sounded "smarmy" and manipulative. I was looking for words and phrases that felt... well ... warmer, friendlier, more honest. Ones that even if the person said no, I wouldn't feel the sting of rejection so bad. Moreover, I wouldn't lose friends if they weren't interested in what I had to offer.

It's the rejection of friends and acquaintances that often paralyzes and/or kills most beginning sales people. "I'm not a salesperson" is a common refrain from people who have been rejected too early in their first attempts at trying to set an appointment or sell something. That's a shame, because almost all of us have to sell something at some point in our lives.

So **I developed a system of setting appointments** (and selling) **that made it almost impossible for people to reject me. It was a way to set an appointment with almost anyone**. Does that mean everyone set an appointment or did business with me every single time? No. Nothing works 100% of the time. But this system worked *almost* 100% of the time, for me.

Through my seminars and coaching, I have made appointment-setting easier and more successful for hundreds of aspiring sales people. Now I feel it is time to put these techniques in writing to help other sales people I can't teach personally. Hence this book you have in your hands.

Let's start by understanding that Prospecting and Setting Appointments are two different skills.

Prospecting

The Art of Finding Potential Clients and Associates

I loved the service I provided. I was excited about presenting it to people because the idea was really beneficial and practically sold itself! There was only one small problem. I was afraid to pick up the phone and ask people for an appointment to show them this exciting idea.

I was always amazed, and at the same time, discouraged by the people in my industry who didn't have any fear of approaching people. They could pick up the phone and cold call out of the phone book. They could walk up to complete strangers, start a conversation, and ask for their name and number and a time to call …

They called it "Prospecting."

I called it "Terror on the Midnight Express."

They had thick skin, and rejection seemed to flow off them like water off a duck's back.

I am the kind of person who walks across the street to avoid talking to people I already know. I was happy being a recluse. Now that I was in sales, I had to actually talk to strangers? Cold call? I was doomed. In an industry full of Lions and Rhinos I felt like a Gopher.

The Lions and Rhinos would go to malls, restaurants, job fairs, any place where they could chat up strangers to interest them in making an appointment. Some even went door to door! They even asked me to go with them! Talk about scary and humiliating!

When I was out shopping, I would see this perfect couple with kids, walking casually in the mall. I would get up my courage to stand in their geographical proximity, and wait for the opportunity to talk to them. Sometimes they would start talking to me!

"Are you from around here? We're looking for the nearest drug store."

I would happily point them in the right direction and watch them smile, thank me, and walk away into the sunset. I could never summon the courage to "prospect" them! Damn it! I am such a LOSER! My colleagues or my wife would ask "Did you get their number?" Each time, embarrassed, I'd have to say no. I HATED prospecting!

On one unsuccessful, and completely miserable, afternoon

I just went home. I pulled out my meager "prospect list" and lamented that I hadn't added any new names to it in over a week.

That's when it dawned on me.

I had names to call on my list already. If I had names on my list that I hadn't called yet, what did I need to get new ones for? If I was too chicken to call people I knew, what did I need new names of complete strangers for?!

Furthermore, as I glanced down the list, I thought of a couple of new names that I had forgotten about. Wait! I just added 2 new names without having to go "malling" and prospecting! I was excited! I thought if I had 50 names on my list, and called 5 a day, that would give me 10 days before I had to start looking for new names! And what if some of those 50 actually wanted to see me and became my client? Maybe they would give me referrals! If I had 10 happy clients that gave me 5 names each I would fill up my prospect list all over again without ever having to do the dreaded prospecting ever again!

So I developed a *new* definition of prospecting:

Prospecting is nothing more than *"putting names on a list."*

Appointment setting is different from prospecting.

Setting Appointments is how you contact those names and arrange a time and place to meet.

Which is a separate skill. If you break the skills up into manageable tasks and learn the steps to each, it makes the whole process of prospecting and setting appointments less onerous.

So if you already have some names on your list, you can skip this chapter and go directly to chapter 4 and work on how to successfully contact and set appointments first. If you run out of names, you can come back to this chapter to learn ways to fill up your list.

For those of you who desperately need a bigger list of names before you can start calling, read on …

Adding Names to your Contact List

I've heard it said that we all know about 450 people. If that's true, and we could contact them all, and set appointments with only 20% of them, that's 90 appointments. Divided over 6 months that's approximately one appointment every working day with weekends off. If 30% did business with you that's 27 new customers. If you earned $1000 per customer that's $27,000 in earnings in 6 months. If you got 5 referrals from each customer, that's another 135 people to call. Chances are, with your increased experience, confidence, and the benefit of happy clients endorsing you, your closing ratio would go up. Your income would naturally follow suit.

That's what happened to me… sort of. I made a list of people I knew from friends, family, school, my wife's friends and family, my former place of work, etc. My list totalled 75 names.

The problem was, I was scared to pick up the phone to call them. I wasn't sure what to say. I was afraid they would say no. I was afraid that I would lose not just an appointment, but possibly a friend who would avoid me. I didn't want to sound like an over-excited, pushy "salesperson". I was afraid that they would laugh and say, I know that stuff already! Or I'm already doing that with a big brand name company, I've never heard of your dumb company!

Most of those fears were made up of course, but they were good enough to paralyze me for hours in front of the phone trying to write "just the right script" and build up enough courage to pick up that 500-pound phone and call someone!

Eventually, as my bank account shrank, and my hunger and desperation grew, I forced myself to start calling those 75 names. It was agonizing, but also exhilarating as I actually started to set, and do, appointments. Some did some business with me and some gave me referrals. Their referrals took me into new markets where I developed different friendships, and centres of influence. Those new friends referred me on to their friends and relatives and so on.

Because I had to keep calling referrals and new contacts every day, just to make a basic living, I actually got better at it and develop my own method for prospecting and setting appointments that actually started to make this "scary task" fun and easy. Not just for me, but for many other aspiring reps, agents and salespeople as my business grew. Today, I have a business that has thousands of clients, and hundreds of agents, seeing hundreds of new families monthly. Yet after almost 29 years, I have never actually contacted the 75th person on my original "Prospect List".

So, whether you believe it or not,

"You Have an Unlimited Market."

If you learn how to set appointments properly, you will be able to,

"Set an appointment with almost anyone."

Therefore, you will always be able to make a living and maybe even make a killing.

"All well and good," you say. "Except, I don't know 450 people. In fact, I only have 10 people on my contact list. And they are all 'tired of hearing from me'. Or, 'I don't know what to say to them', or I've called them and they said, 'Not right now' or 'I'm busy' or 'I've already got what you are offering,' etc., etc., etc."

Sometimes just staring at your meagre contact list paralyzes you to the point where you don't contact them for fear of "not having anyone left on your list." You would be out of business! So you just keep your list as a souvenir of hope like a family heirloom on your mantle-piece, collecting dust.

It's like opening your refrigerator looking for something easy, convenient and savoury to eat and seeing nothing readily available. So you shut the door. But you are still hungry so you open it up and look again. Still nothing. You may even do that two or three more times. Waiting for something delicious to magically appear that's easy to eat. Damn it. Still Nothing. But you are starving! How come there's no supper on the table?! How comes there's no food in my fridge?! How come no one got groceries?! How come I'm still single?! Can you relate? No? It's probably just a guy thing.

So now, you have a problem. You are starving and there's nothing in your fridge that's easily edible. So you have two choices: Go grocery shopping or get creative with the food you have in the fridge and cook something!

Same as your prospect list. You keep staring at it hoping a name will pop out at you that is an easy one to call. An easy appointment, a sure client that will make you some money! Because you are broke! But there's nothing "easily edible or sellable" on your prospect list. So you have two choices: Go get some more names, or get creative with the names you have and make an appointment with them! (See chapter 5.)

But for now, let's just go grocery shopping and fill up your fridge. I mean your list.

Bearing in mind the definition of prospecting is **"Putting names on a list"**…

1. Make an appointment with yourself for 45 minutes.

2. Pull out your contact list or a note pad where you can create a contact list.

3. Open your contact list on your cell phone or paper phone list. Go down your list and take names that you want to call off that list and write (yes, write) them on your separate prospect/contact list.

4. Open your calendar (electronic or paper). Starting from last week, go back through it and look for names you have forgotten about. Go back as far as you can in the time you have allotted yourself for this task (45 minutes).

    Did you add any names to your list? (It's like looking into the far reaches of your fridge and finding a savoury "left over". Yum! You gleefully devour it to satisfy your hunger.)

    Sometimes you stumble across that great prospect

on your list that told you they were interested but had put you off and you forgot about her. You gleefully pick up the phone and set an easy appointment to satisfy your hunger for a sale.

But DON'T DO THAT YET! Resist the temptation to make that call until you get to Chapter 4. I will explain why later. Suffice to say for now, **"you can't fix problems with the same habits that created them in the first place."** Putting it another way… if your fridge is chronically empty … **It's not the fridge's fault.**

Another refrigerator analogy before we move on….

Have you ever looked into the far reaches of your fridge and found mouldy leftovers? What do you do? Ladies, you throw it out immediately, don't you? In fact you look at the expiry date and throw things out before they get mouldy. Guys will take the lid off, look inside, smell it, then cut off the mouldy parts and eat the "non-mouldy" parts if they are really hungry, or really lazy, or really broke. I know. It's Gross. Guys! Just throw that stuff out and clean your fridge before it becomes a science experiment! Remember how much you enjoyed science in high school? Oh wait, you didn't enjoy it. That's why you are in sales.

Your prospect list has mouldy leads on it as well. You know… the ones that keep putting you "OFF", or you have approached them incorrectly and turned them "OFF"… or prospects that actually turn you "OFF" at the thought of even having to call them *again*! But you keep them on your list cause they are "easy" to call or they might say yes one day. Do yourself a favour! Get them "OFF" your prospect list! Same as you should throw out mouldy leftovers in your fridge. Throw them out! If you honestly think you can scrape the mould off and contact them, then do it! Set an appointment or get them off your list before they morph into an experiment in career ending frustration!

But again, don't contact your "leads" yet. Wait till the next chapter. For now, we are just cleaning out the fridge and "restocking it with *fresh* food". Doesn't just the thought of that make you *feel* better?

5. If you have an old *Yellow Pages* phone book, open it up to the beginning. (Or go online to "Prospect Memory Jogger - Comcast.net) I mean NOW. Go get the *Yellow Pages* out or pull up the Memory Jogger website! Do it! Start writing down all names that come to mind as you glance through the headings: Accountants (what about yours?), Aircraft (know anybody who works at an airport?), Auto body repair (who fixed your last fender bender?), Barber, Beauty Salons (your hairdresser), Carpet Cleaners (do you plan on getting your carpets cleaned? the cleaners are in your house for a couple of hours…), Car Dealers (who did you buy or lease your last car from?) …

In fact anyone who you bought something from recently is a potential appointment. If nothing else, they should feel somewhat obligated to return the favour.

Keep going through the *Yellow Pages* headings for 45 minutes to an hour. If you have lived in your area for 2 years or longer I defy you to get past "E" without writing down an additional 25 to 30 names. Try it. Seriously, put this book down and just try it! Keep going through the alphabetical listings until you have 75 to 100 names.

You may not even know their name. Just write down "guy who fixed my car." "Lady I met at the airport kiosk." "Gas station convenience store attendant," etc.

Don't worry about how to approach them yet. Just keep adding names to your list. Fill it up! Fill your fridge!

Once you have a "full" "refreshed" list, doesn't that *feel* better? You suddenly have a lot more potential people to call! You actually prospected in the comfort of your own home and it took less than an hour! Please tell yourself: ***I have an unlimited market!*** You'll never run out of people to call! There's always more! More babies being born! More kids graduating from high school and college, more people getting married, more people moving into your area, more changing jobs, retiring, and having grandkids!

Once you have a bigger list, you don't feel so much of the pressure of using up all your names. Even if you screw up the first couple calls, who cares?! You have dozens and dozens more to call! And you will get better at setting appointments! Even if you're lousy at it to begin with, I guarantee someone will surprise you and say, "Sure, I'd love to get together and chat with you."

I will also guarantee this: No calls = No appointments.

6.   "Don't go prospecting – prospect as you go."

The bad news about not having any appointments is, well, you don't have any appointments. But the good news is, not having any appointments gives you time to "Prospect as you go." What do I mean by that? Without a lot of appointments to take up your day or evening, you are free to go and do things that you enjoy and even meet people that enjoy the same things you do! Hello! New friends? Even if they are complete strangers, people that like the same things you do have something in common with you! They instantly qualify as "cool" market contacts. All you have to do is warm them up to warm market contacts.

How to do that is explained in the next chapter.

Warming Up the Cool Market

The Art of Turning Strangers into Prospects

During Christmas break after my first semester of Aviation College, I opened a letter from the department head notifying me that **I was on probation**.

What!?

How could that be?! I had been one of only 27 applicants out of 400 to be accepted into this program and now they were telling me I was on probation after one semester?! What for?!

"Mr. Andruschak, your 1st term mark in Calculus is a C-. In order to continue in the Aviation program you must maintain a C+ average. If you do not bring your grade in Calculus up to a C+ by the end of the next term, you will have to withdraw from the Aviation program."

I was devastated! I started to see all my dreams of becoming an airline pilot slip away. No flying big jets to exotic places in the world, no six-figure salary with lots of time off, no cool uniform, no cute flight attendants! What the heck! All because I got a C- in Calculus?! What does that have to do with flying, for crying out loud?!

I didn't think Calculus mattered as much as my flying courses so I hadn't developed the attention to detail that the calculations required which caused me to make dumb mistakes and do poorly on tests. Besides that, I kept telling myself that I hated Math, as most people do. And because I hated it, I avoided spending any real time studying it. Hence my C-, and now probation!

But I had no time for a pity party. I cut my Christmas break short, and headed back to school early to talk to my Calculus prof.

I was grateful that he made the time to meet with me and talk about the love he had for Calculus. He explained how Isaac Newton had discovered it and how it is used to help understand the laws of the universe, and economics of countries, and science of life. I was in awe. It was then I committed to start at least to "like Calculus" and spend time every day studying it. By the end of the next semester, my mark went from C- to a B+! I really did develop a "love" for Calculus that I still have today.

I believe **Prospecting and Setting Appointments is a lot like the "Math" of a salesperson's career**.

Very few of us are good at it, and even fewer really enjoy doing it. Therefore, most of us never spend the necessary time every day to get good at it. The result is often below average earnings, being put on probation by their company (or their spouse), and ultimately, failure to accomplish their goals.

My goal in this book, is to make you at least "like" the process of prospecting and making calls. If you at least get rid of the aversion to the activity, and spend time "studying" it every day, you too can turn your below average income into above average earnings in a "semester", or about 90 to 120 days.

The strategy for improving my Calculus grade, and the process for improving your grade in Prospecting and Setting Appointments are very similar.

1. **Find books, recordings, webcasts, etc., of people who like to prospect.** Listen to these people often. Their enthusiasm is infectious.

2. **Commit some time everyday to prospect and make calls. Preferably the same time every day.** But no more than 45 minutes to an hour. In fact, start with just 20 minutes every other day. (I developed a true understanding of short, concentrated, but consistent, 20 minutes of effort after reading "Body for Life" by Bill Phillips. In 12 weeks I transformed my lethargic, out-of-shape body, into a triathlon-ready athlete without gimmicks. Just good diet and focussed exercise. I believe the same fundamentals can be applied to your sales career.)

3. **Study the techniques. Have patience with the details.** Just like a misplaced "+" or "-" sign can cause errors that

fail Math tests, a misplaced or forgotten word can cause failure when making phone calls to prospective clients.

So let's begin.

We can divide our market into 4 categories:

HOT, WARM, COOL and COLD.

Hot Market are people who LOVE you

- Your partner, and closest family and friends
- They will definitely set an appointment with you even if they are skeptical of your offering.

Warm Market are people who LIKE you

- Classmates, co-workers, teammates, etc.
- They will most often set an appointment with you if you approach them correctly. If you approach them incorrectly they may become suspicious and skeptical and not set an appointment with you. You have essentially "cooled off" your warm market.

Cool Market are people who you have something in common with.

- They will initially be skeptical and will be unlikely to set an appointment with you, especially if you approach them incorrectly.
- These people should be "warmed up" first.

Cold Market are people that you have nothing in common with or you have pissed them off.

- They will not set an appointment with you. Unless, you have to be lucky enough to catch them at the exact right time that they are desperately looking for what you have to offer. That's why "telemarketers" even get results in Cold markets. But they have to have incredibly thick skin and a process to navigate around Federal Do Not Call Lists. Good luck with that.

Obviously the more Hot Market and Warm Market people you know, the more appointments you will set. If you want to develop more of those types of relationships you have to learn **How to Warm Up the Cool Market**:

Step One:
Get your butt out of the hut

As in the previous chapter, if you have few, or no, appointments, then you have time to get your "butt out of your hut" and do things you enjoy. While out and about, try to enjoy meeting new people. Don't worry about talking to them about your business. Just enjoy the process of "Friendship Farming," and becoming a "Fisher of Men" (and Women). Notice the terms *fishing* and *farming* – not *hunting* and *killing*.

This is not a race to meet people to make sales. It's an opportunity to meet people that may become friends first, and possibly clients second.

"But, Barry," you say, "I'm broke and don't have time for this farming/fishing stuff! I need sales and money now!"

Well then, get a job that pays a salary, not a commission. Real long-term success in sales takes time. The bad reputation that sales people get is from the "pushiness" that people feel from someone who is desperate to make money or meet a quota.

The goal here is to try to build up your market and develop

clients who **like you and trust you** and will refer people to you. Not to make your friends and acquaintances cross the street to avoid talking to you.

So if you don't have a Warm Market, be prepared to give this process a minimum of 90 days. Warming up the Cool Market, or developing a new Warm Market list of people to call takes about 3 months. That doesn't mean you won't get any appointments or sales in 3 months, it means that building a new Warm market and the momentum of **regular referrals** and **consistent appointments and sales** takes about 90 to 120 days.

Step Two:
Go to where people are

Sporting events. Craft shows, school functions, parks, beaches, parties, concerts, open houses, garage sales, etc. But think of places you enjoy. I like airplanes so I go to small airports. If you like soccer, join a team or watch your kids play. Go to a bar to watch football, or to the rink to watch hockey. Go shopping, or to the art gallery, or the marina if you like boats, or car lots if you like cars, or to home shows or open houses if you like looking at real estate.

None of this has to cost money. But you can still shop, and dream a little. You may not be able to buy the dream car or home today, but have the attitude or belief that next year or the year after … you might.

For instance, when we were 27, my wife and I started to dream house shop for an oceanfront home in a sought after neighbourhood. The prices of these homes were out of most people's reach that had steady jobs in their 40's and 50's let alone two people in their 20's who lived on commission. So realtors weren't even willing to show us those kind of homes.

But we kept looking and dreaming anyway. We actually found one we liked at a price we could afford. In the meantime, after I worked my prospecting and appointment setting plan for over 2 years, we had saved a big down payment and actually got pre-approved for a large mortgage with our bank. We shocked everyone when we bought that oceanfront home within 6 months after dreaming about it. The realtors and others who believed in us also became my clients. So did the guy I bought my BMW from! ... and the parts manager and service manager, and their friends and family too!

So don't stop believing is the moral of that *journey*.

(Get it? The song *"Don't Stop Believing"* is by the band Journey? I'm sure you got that, but incidentally, the husband and wife team that recruited and trained me in my financial services business used to be in Steve Perry's band in Tulare, California. But they quit before Steve became famous with Journey. Maybe they stopped "believing." Steve Perry obviously did not. And neither should you.)

Step Three:
Master the art of idle conversation, or "Breaking the Ice"

This did not come naturally to me. I hated idle conversation. But I had to learn how to do it. So I started with just *looking people in the eye, smiling*, and saying: "Hi, how is the day going?" or "Nice day today, huh?" or "Day off today?" or "Are those your kids?" or "Are you the manager (owner) here?"

By breaking the ice, while in an elevator, a line up, or anywhere you are in the proximity of people, you would be surprised how some people just start talking to you. Especially if you don't have an agenda about "trying to sell them something" or feeling the pressure of "having to interest them in your business," etc. Just try and enjoy the "art of idle conversation."

Step Four:
Listen, and ask questions to keep them talking

Yep. Listen. Ask questions. Keep them talking. The old adage "two ears, one mouth, use them in that proportion" still applies. The more people feel heard and listened to, **the more they begin to like you** – the more they "warm up." Ask questions centred around things that interest *them*, not just you. When it comes time to call for an appointment, you may be amazed at their lack of resistance and willingness to see you. Why? Because they remember how much they enjoyed talking to you and want the experience to continue! Most people have an incredibly strong need to be heard. They may even know that you are trying to "prospect" them but are still willing to see you because they have come to **like you** at least enough to give you 20 to 30 minutes of their time! And, that's all you need if you are good with your presentation.

The key element of **trust** is built quickly through the next step.

Step Five:
Find common ground

Look for areas of mutual interest and rapport. For example, similar background and neighbourhood, common friends, similar age children in same school or activity, what they do for a living. If you are in a bookstore, talk about books. If at a sporting event, talk about the team. If you're at a party, ask how they know the host, etc., etc. But make sure 75% of the time it's about THEM. For more on this, read Dale Carnegie's *"How to Win Friends and Influence People"* or google "How to get people to like you in 90 seconds or less" at www.wikiHow.com. **The more commonality you discover the more they begin to trust you.**

Warning: If you have a difficulty warming people up and eventually getting appointments and developing clients even after all this training, it's probably because you have not worked hard enough to cultivate a personality that people **like and trust**. Are you too loud and obnoxious? Are you too socially awkward? Do you dress too provocatively (ladies) or too weird (guys)? Do you have bad breath or are you having a bad hair decade? Seriously. Maybe it's time for a makeover.

I read *"Dress for Success"* for men 30 years ago to learn how to make a great first impression on a budget. I followed that book's advice, bought two suits, two white shirts and two ties and wore the same thing every day for two years. At least I felt confident that I wasn't turning people off with how I dressed. Believe me, people notice those things. Especially women. Now you can google all that stuff. So do it. My car was a beater, but I didn't sit at their kitchen table with my car. I parked my POS (guys, you know what that stands for – piece of s#*t) down the street so they couldn't see me drive up, or drive away. People judge you by the car you drive. Especially men.

Those first two suits that I paid good money for, however, made me thousands of dollars. With those thousands of dollars, I bought a new car … with cash. But, I only did that after I maxed out my emergency fund and retirement savings account. (Read *"The Wealthy Barber"* by David Chilton who is currently on *"Dragon's Den".*)

When you are in sales, in our society, what you drive and and how you dress does help to **build trust** or break trust. Just saying.

Step Six:
Know how to explain what you do

Know the answer to *"What is it that you do?"* Make it sound non-threatening, but interesting.

"I work for ABC company. We specialize in helping families get out of debt and free up money to invest. What do you do?"

Try to avoid the temptation of doing a "presentation" about your business when someone simply asks what you do. Just turn the situation around for a minute. You are at a party and you ask somebody what they do and they go into a complete presentation about their business. You begin to assume they're trying to promote their business or sell you something which, in a social situation, can be a put off. If they ask you to elaborate about what you do then fine, go ahead and explain your business. But again, remember to ask them questions to get them talking more than you talk.

Step Seven:
Ask for contact info in a sincere and friendly way

Have a nice way to exchange numbers if the opportunity arises.

"I have to run, but maybe we could continue our conversation or discuss this further over coffee?"

"Listen, I have to get to my next meeting, but perhaps we can exchange numbers and do some networking over coffee some time?"

"Can we exchange numbers and I will text you?"

"Do you have a card? Perhaps we can sit down for coffee and exchange ideas at some point."

"If you are in need of some advice on that I'd be happy to stay in touch. I may need your service at some point as well."

"Why don't we exchange numbers and I will call you next week? Perhaps I can answer some of your questions over the phone or in-person if you like."

The list is endless. Even if you don't ask for their number right away, that's okay. Just get comfortable with conversations that "warm up the cool market" and the numbers and contacts will come your way.

If they do give you their number, add that name to your list of people to call in the next week or two. Congratulations! You have successfully prospected! Even if you just get a name and where they work, you may be able to look up their work number and call them there, if appropriate.

The bottom line is contained in the some of the bold type in the previous paragraphs in case you hadn't noticed – getting people to **like you and trust you**. If you are already a likeable and trustworthy person, but a little introverted and shy, try those tips and you will have more appointments than you can handle.

Setting Appointments

The Art of Creating Face-to-Face Meetings with Potential Clients and Associates

As a young boy, I used to love fishing for trout in the nearby creek. I got pretty good at the technique of catching small fish. Trying to catch 20 lb salmon from a boat, however, required a completely different set of skills. The first time I went salmon fishing, my dad hired two guides and two small boats. One for him and his buddy, and one for me, and my buddy. But according to Dad's guide, "No one is catching fish so far today."

That comment just added to my nervousness. I thought, *if I only get one bite, I better not lose it because I may not get another one.* But the younger guide in our boat told us, "Don't worry, guys, we are going to max out today."

Really, I thought? I wasn't sure if I believed him fully. But his comment did make me relax a bit and look forward to the experience.

Next the guide showed us how to make a "cut plug." This means preparing a herring on the right hook so when we trolled, it looked as if the herring was swimming.

Then he said to watch the tip of the rod for a certain type of "bend." When you see that, pick up your rod from the holder, wait till the line started to spin off the reel, then "tap" your thumb on the spinning reel to slow it, which sets the hook in the salmon's mouth. Once you have one on the line, reel him in until he wants to run, let the reel spin, but don't let the line go slack. Keep reeling, letting him run, and reeling him in until he tires out and gets close enough to the boat where the guide could net him.

"Don't jerk the rod up too hard or fast, and don't let the line go slack," he repeated a number of times.

Much to everyone's surprise, we maxed out that day. In other words, on a day when no one was catching salmon, my friend and I caught 3 each! Dad and his friend got skunked and had to settle for jigging a halibut.

Beginners luck? Maybe. But that experience taught me a lot. Not just about salmon fishing, but how to be a fisher of men (and women). I applied those techniques to the very important skills of prospecting and appointment setting.

So here are the steps to successfully getting a potential client "in the boat" so to speak. These steps are described in the same detail that the fishing guide taught me... right down to the

all-important "tapping the thumb on the reel" to set the hook. We will also learn how to professionally follow up by "letting them run without letting the line go slack."

And don't worry. We are going to max out today. And every day from now on, if you like.

Preparing to Make the Call

Each one of these steps is explained in detail in chapter 5. But if you are anxious to just get calling, this chapter will help you get started. I used to tape these steps to my office wall to motivate me to make calls and remind me how to get started correctly. Another tip is to use voice note on your smart phone to record these tips for yourself to play over and over again in your car as you drive.

1. Pick five names from your Hot or Warm list.

2. Write down the easiest one to call first, the hardest one to call last. (Yes, write them down.)

3. Have your agenda open and know when you want to meet.

4. Keep score, "the Serious Money" way.

5. Choose your script.

6. Replace images of fear with images of success.

7. Get motivated – music, motivational video or speech, etc.

Making the Calls

1. Dial the full 10 digit number. Don't hang up if some-one answers.

2. If they answer, introduce yourself saying, *"Hi Bob, **it's** Joe Smith calling."*

3. Tell them where you know them from (if you are calling your cool market).

4. Ask if you have caught them at a bad time.

5. If they answer yes (you have caught them at a bad time), ask permission to call back in an hour or *"Would tomor-row be better?"*

6. If *no* (meaning you haven't caught them at a bad time and they are free to talk) state the reason for your call – your script…for example *(stating the name of your com-pany and the benefit of your offering quickly and concisely)*: *"The reason I'm calling is I work with ABC company, we have a program that has helped lots of people reduce taxes, free up additional money to save, and improve the rate of return on their investments. But… **are you locked in to what you are doing right now** financially, **or are you open to suggestions?"***

7. If they respond positively, **ask for an appointment** of-fering them an alternative of choice so they don't feel pressured. For example,

"So IF we were to get together to discuss it further, would this week or next week be better?

Early in the week or later in the week?

Daytimes or evenings? Weekdays or weekends, 6 or 8 pm …"

8. If they are "locked in," thank them for their time and say if they ever change their mind to please give you a call.

9. If lukewarm, use the indirect approach.

10. Reward yourself *after* you make your 5 calls.

So your call would go something like this:

"Hi Bob, it's Joe Smith calling, we met at the parent teacher meeting last Wednesday. Have I caught you at a bad time?"

"Oh hi, Joe. No. Go ahead."

"Great, well the reason I am calling is I work with a company called ABC, and we specialize in helping people reduce taxes, free up money to save, and help them get higher returns on their investments.

But are you locked into what you are doing right now financially, or are you open to suggestions?"

(If you are in the recruiting business, your script would go like this: "I work for ABC company that is expanding in the area and they are looking for some key people. I thought you might be the kind of people they are looking for. But are you locked in to what you are doing right now, career wise (job wise), or are you open to looking at other things?)

"I'm always open."

"Great. If we were to get together for 20 or 30 minutes to chat, would this week or next week be better for you?"

"Next week is better."

"Daytime or evening?"

"Evening."

"Okay, how about Thursday evening about 7 pm?"

"That's fine."

"At your house or would you prefer to meet at a coffee shop?"

"If you can come to the house that would be great."

"Okay, what's your address?"

"1234 Alpha Street."

"Would you like your wife to be there as well?"

"Sure."

"Okay, I have about 30 minutes worth of ideas to show you. If any of them pique your interest and you have questions, I'll stay longer. If not, I will be on my way. Either way, it will be nice to chat with you. Sound okay?"

(Recruiting business: Okay, It will take me about 20 minutes to show you a little bit about who we are, what we do, what's in it for you. If it piques your interest, we can continue talking. If it's not for you, maybe you can point me in the right direction. Sound fair?)

"Yeah, that sounds fine."

"Great. I'll text (or call) you Wednesday just to see if 7 pm Thursday still works. Or you can text me, here's my number: 250-xxx-xxxx. Look forward to seeing you then. Thanks, Bob."

Now obviously they don't all go like that. But you would be surprised how many of them do. My personal experience as well as the experience of hundreds of other reps I have coached is that if they actually ask 5 people in their warm market for an appointment, 1 or 2 will say *yes* just like that. Only 1 out 5 or 10 actually say *no*. The rest are *maybe's* or *not-right-now's*.

Handling a NO

No. No, thank you. No, I've changed my mind. No, I don't want any. No. No time. No money. No, you are ugly and your mom dresses you funny. No. NO.

The NO. So destructive of the average salesperson's career that the great sales trainer Tom Hopkins devoted a whole chapter to it in his classic "How to Master the Art of Selling."

If you do get a NO on your appointment setting attempt it will usually sound something like this:

"Yes, I am pretty locked in (committed) to what I'm doing right now (financially, career wise, service wise, etc)."

Wait.

In order to say NO to the appointment setting script "are you locked in," they had to say YES. Mmmmm. That didn't feel so bad, did it?

Here's how to respond:

"I thought you may be (pretty busy, well looked after in that area, already have an advisor, etc.), Bob, but would you mind if I popped by one day to buy you a cup of coffee, and show you what I'm doing, and the kind of people I'm looking for... perhaps you can point me in the right direction? (or perhaps you could refer me on to someone who could use my services down the road?) Would that be okay?"

"Sure. I could do that."

"Great. So IF we were to get together for coffee, would this week or next be better for you?"

And so on.

Can you imagine that most salespeople are paralyzed simply by the thought that they may get one NO? When, statistically, only about 10% to 20% of appointment setting attempts result in someone actually saying NO, and 20 to 40% say YES!

So this strategy minimizes the effect of a NO if you get one, and allows you to focus on the YESSES! Less rejection, more success keeps a rep on the phone and on appointments more often. Isn't that what we all want?!

"Maybe's and not-right-now's"

What about the other 50 to 60% of appointment setting attempts that don't say yes or no, just "not right now, I'm too busy … maybe after the summer. Can you email me something?"

Here is your general answer: "Okay, no problem, Bob, I thought you may be pretty busy this time of year. So do I have your permission to follow up with you? (…in a month, at the end of the summer, after your daughter's wedding, after you get the email?)"

"Sure."

"Alright, we'll chat then. Thanks for taking the call."

Now we are into the realm of the follow-up which will be covered in detail in Chapter 6. But before we deal with follow up, its important to fully understand the Psychology and Reasoning behind this Setting Appointment Formula.

Understanding the Power of Persuasion

The Psychology and Reasoning
Behind the Appointment Setting Formula

The Power to Persuade can be an enormous force for good if used with the right motives. Having the wrong motives on the other hand, can turn the power to persuade into a negative force just as easily. Persuading people to do things that are solely in your best interest, not theirs, is manipulation. But persuading people to do what is in *their* best interest, and maybe yours as well, is positive. So if you have a good, honest product that you sincerely believe benefits others, then it is vital to fully understand the power of persuasion. But before you can become proficient at persuading others to set an appointment, you first have to become proficient at *persuading yourself to make the calls.*

To help you with that, here is the important rationale and psychology behind this appointment setting method:

Preparing to Make Calls

Preparing to make the call is as important as *making* the call itself.

Why? Because it helps *reduce rejection*. Not eliminate it, but reduce it to the point that will generate more success over time, with less mental effort. It stands to reason that if you can reduce the fear and rejection associated with a task, you will do more of it. Hence by shear weight of the increase in number of attempts, you will succeed where others have failed. So let's figure out why this system works the way it does.

1.   **Take five names from your Hot or Warm list.** Why five names? It is not too many, or too few, names to call. And it often generates at least one or maybe two appointments with only small amounts of rejection. A **Big Mistake** people often make is getting motivated to call "this one" person. After the call they may get an appointment, which is exciting, but they waste all that excitement and success on one call. If they had at least 5 to call, the motivation may carry them through to set another one and/or deal more effectively with a *maybe* or a *no*. So, do yourself a favour. When you're motivated to call, pick at least 5 names. Another **Big Mistake** is trying to call too many all at once. To me that's like being a bull in a china shop. Even if you have a thick skin, it's still too much potential for rejection

and disorganization of scripts, agendas, etc. Spreading the calls out over a week or two is more effective.

2. **List the easiest one to call first, the hardest one to call last**. If you are attempting a difficult task, or something you have been avoiding, it is psychologically beneficial to start easy. The easiest chore, the easiest debt to pay off, the lightest weight to lift, the shortest, easiest cardio exercise, or task, to start with. It just makes it easier to get over the mental resistance of actually just starting the task or exercise program, at all. This is critical. *The easiest call should be to a person that **you do not care** whether they say yes or no.*

3. **Have your agenda open and know when you want to meet.** Even though the outcome of the phone call is both uncertain and somewhat out of your control, being certain of when you are able to meet creates a small confidence by feeling that you actually do have some control over your schedule and your life. **Big Mistake**: actually getting an appointment and booking it right on top of the only other appointment you had that week! Now you may have to reschedule one of them and risk sounding unprofessional and never getting a re-schedule. All because you didn't check your agenda first. Dumb Dumb.

4. **Keep score**, the "Serious Money" way. *"Serious Money"* is a book written by the fabled, Mutual Fund Marketing Guru, Nick Murray. In it he explained that

all successful sales had a ratio of appointments to phone calls. In other words, how many calls do you need to make to get one appointment? In my world it is one to two appointments from every five calls. Your ratios may be different but it's important to keep track of calls made, and appointments set, for three reasons. First, it is a small reward/reinforcement for doing the activity. Second, it proves to you that you will get appointments for a given number of calls. In other words, "hard work pays off." Third, by keeping track of your activity, it proves that you actually did work, the results are measurable, and you can show to other sales people that consistently making calls yields consistent results. It is the "Law of large numbers" that makes the "Law of averages" possible. By consistently making a certain number of calls every week for 8 to 12 weeks you will see miraculous changes in your business life. But if you don't keep track, you'll encounter a no-appointment week or two because all you have been making is follow-up calls, no new calls. You will lose your appointment setting "rhythm" and have to start all over again. **Big Mistake**.

5. **Choose your script**. Different prospects require different scripts. Make sure you decide what script would work best with a prospect *before* they answer the phone! You may still not be right, but you increase your chances of being successful if you prepare ahead of time.

6. **Replace images of fear with images of success.** Before

I picked up the phone to call my first prospect, the old "what if" fear would set in. What if he or she was already a happy client of someone else? What if they just had a fight with their spouse or boss and were just waiting to take it out on me? What if they knew more about the product or service I was offering and laughed at my feeble attempt at educating them? None of those fears are rational, of course. I was making them up. So one day I thought if I'm making fears up, why couldn't I make up successes as well? So I started to replace images of fear with images of success. And it worked! I did not know at that time that I was invoking the powerful "Law of Attraction." There are now hundreds, if not thousands, of books on this subject. But I will explain how this vital concept is applied to appointment setting in a later chapter.

7. **Get motivated** – music, motivational video or speech, etc. My favourite was *"Start Me Up"* by the Rolling Stones. Same as # 6 but using external "feel good" mechanisms to jump-start the "Law of Attraction." **Big Mistake**: going to a motivational event or watching or listening to something exciting and NOT having your 5 names immediately ready to call. Motivation and "feel good" moments are fleeting. Don't squander them. Take action!

Now you have learned a formula for persuading yourself to do the most important part of the sales process. The one that everyone avoids. Now you can work on persuading others.

The Psychology behind Making the Calls

1. **Dial the full 10-digit phone number.** It's amazing how many 9-digit phone #'s there are. And none of them work. Have some guts. Punch in the full ten digits. Smart phones with full numbers to enter by the name eliminate this somewhat, but the point is – let the phone ring until someone answers or you get a message.

    Texting is often more effective than a phone call these days. But it is better for contacting people in your hot or warm market, or for follow-ups than for initial calls to your cool market, in my opinion. However, if I am trying to set an actual appointment, I do need to talk to them by phone. So I may text someone simply asking, "Can I call you?" If the answer is yes, then I can launch into my script over the phone.

2. **Intro yourself.** If they answer, say *"Hi Bob, it's Joe Smith calling."* "It's" is warmer than "This Is." "It's" makes it sound like they should know you. It opens them up more, versus closing them down and making them wary.

3. **Tell them where you know them from** (if you are calling cool or warm market). People are generally suspicious for the first few seconds of a phone call that they aren't expecting. Telling them fairly quickly how they know you makes them less suspicious.

4. **Ask if you have caught them at a bad time.** Nothing

defeats the good intentions of a call more than a rambling caller catching someone in the middle of a meeting, dinner, rushing out somewhere, etc. Has that ever happened to you? Annoying, isn't it? Remember, you are trying to warm up the contact, not cool them off. So always ask if you caught them at a bad time to give them a chance to say *yes*. They will appreciate the professional courtesy. Because you used the words *Have I caught you at a bad time?* it subtly uses reverse psychology, often compelling people to say *no*. Which is actually an affirmation for you to go ahead. *No* actually becomes a yes. And you start looking forward to hearing a no. How cool is that?

5. **If they answer *yes*** (you have caught them at a bad time, which is actually a *no* but doesn't feel like a rejection because they actually said *yes*), ask permission to call back in an hour or *"Would tomorrow be better?"* Wait for the response then put it in your agenda and alarm it so you don't forget. Calling someone back if they ask you to is a mark of professionalism that only adds to your credibility. Not calling back, of course, has the opposite effect.

6. **If they answer *no*** (meaning you haven't caught them at a bad time and they are free to talk), state the reason for your call – your script… Some small talk here may be okay, but try to get to the point as soon as possible. For example, *"The reason I'm calling is I have a program that*

(fill in the blanks with your own script) has helped lots of people reduce taxes, free up additional money to save, and improve the rate of return on their investments. But are you locked in to what you are doing right now financially, or are you open to suggestions?" The phrase "locked in" is similar to "have I caught you at a bad time." It compels people to say "no" (which, again, is an affirmation) because most people don't want to admit they are "locked in" to anything. If that word doesn't work for you, replace it with "committed."

7. If they respond positively, usually by saying "I'm always open," **ask for an appointment**, offering them an alternative of choice so they don't feel pressured.

    For example, *"So IF we were to get together to discuss it further, would this week or next week be better?"*

    "Early in the week or later in the week?"

    "Daytimes or evenings?"

    "Weekdays or weekends, 6 or 8 pm ... " The word **"IF"** is one of the best transition words in the English language. It's as subtly powerful as when I learned to catch salmon by tapping my thumb on the fishing reel. It gives people a chance to venture forward toward exploring the benefits of a commitment without actually making one. **I believe people have difficulty making decisions and commitments but love to have choices and options.** The "if" word, followed by a couple of choices, gives people what they want. The feeling that they are in control of their choices instead of being

pushed for a commitment or a decision that they typically aren't 100% ready to make. *And it's really hard to say no to someone who offers you choices without pressure.* Especially if the product or service is something they are at least mildly interested in. ***Let me repeat that: it's really hard to say no to someone who offers you choices without pressure.* Especially if the product or service is something they are at least mildly interested in.**

8. If they are "locked in," thank them for their time and say if they ever change their mind to please give you a call.

9. If lukewarm, use the **indirect approach**. Indirect means you call them in an effort to ask their help to refer you to someone they know. For instance: *"I know you may not be interested yourself, but you may know just the person I could talk to."* Or: *"I was wondering if I could take 20 minutes of your time to show you what I do and the kind of people I am looking for and perhaps you could point me in the right direction."* Or: *"I was hoping if I showed you exactly what it is that I do, you could refer me on to people that may need my services at some point in the future."*

10. **Reward yourself** after you make your 5 calls. This is a critical, yet often overlooked, step in conditioning yourself to do what you know you need to do, but have been avoiding. *Can you hear yourself procrastinating with these lines: "I will make my calls AFTER I have a coffee,*

or after my work out, or after lunch, etc, etc, etc." Try to use your caffeine addiction, or your hunger pains, as a trigger to make your calls first! Then, use those daily pleasures as a reward for making the calls! Eventually, the calls lead to a pleasure response in the brain, because as soon as you are done, you get to have that special lunch, or donut, or latte you were craving. Now that's the kind of "latte factor" that actually puts money into your pocket for retirement instead of just taking money out! (Thank you, David Bach, for that tip from his classic book, *"The Automatic Millionaire".*)

If you follow all those steps often enough to form a new habit, you may actually begin to "love the Math" part of a sales career. Loving an activity will cause you to spend more time doing it. Spending more time on the critical part of generating sales, will set you apart from the rest. It will bring your below-average "C-" earnings up to "B+" or even excellent earnings.

Then you can truly enjoy the things in life that others can't ... until they are willing to do the work that you did!

6

Follow-up

The Art of Being Pleasantly Persistent
with People Who Postpone

It's been my experience that most appointments postpone at least once. So the excellent rep prepares for that by having a plan B, C and often D. In other words, If client 'A' postpones on short notice, you need a few alternate clients that you can slot in to the postponed time slot. That way you can minimize the frustration of last minute postponements by having lots of follow ups that may be able to fill in on short notice.

For example, Client A postpones on short notice because of an unforeseen conflict with a child's sporting event.

"Sorry for the short notice, Barry, but my son's coach

scheduled an extra practice that I have to get him to tonight. Can we postpone till next week?"

"Sure Bob, no prob. (lol) This time next week, okay?"

"Yah, that's great Thanks for your flexibility. See you next week."

Now you have an opening for a 6:30 appointment to fill.

Geographical Proximity Close

Here's a tip: Look down your follow-up list for someone who lives in the same geographical area that you are on or going to be in at 6:30. Then try this:

"Hi Sue, it's Barry Andruschak calling. Have I caught you in the middle of dinner?"

"No, Barry, go ahead."

"I have that information you wanted and it actually requires about 15 minutes of explanation. I'm going to be in your area this evening about 6:30-ish. May I pop by and drop it to you rather than emailing it?"

"Well if you're in the area, sure pop by. We have to head out by 7 though."

"Okay, no prob. See you at 6:30."

Or actually go to the area your potential client lives or works in before you make your follow up call.

Call or text: Hey Sue, I'm just at (corner of, coffee shop, mall, street, in their neighbourhood) and have about an hour before my next meeting, just thought I'd see if you had a few minutes for me to drop that brochure to you.

Its amazing how many times people who have been

postponing you, will be available on short notice especially if you are in their neighbourhood.

Even if don't have another appointment in an hour, say you do anyway. It makes people think you are busy (and therefore important) and it also ensures in their mind that you won't be camped out at their kitchen table all night.

Which, by the way is one of the main reason people postpone your attempt at a second appointment in the first place... your first presentation took WAY longer than you said it would. Another reason to keep your first presentation to 20 -30 minutes max.

Another tip

If you get a short notice postponement for tonight (let's say Monday night), look further down your week for a client you could move from, say, Thursday night to tonight. They may even appreciate seeing you sooner as well. Why is this a good Plan B? Because, if you can move a Thursday to fill a Monday, it frees up a slot on Thursday now and gives you 3 days to fill it. Giving yourself and your contacts 3 days notice is easier than trying to ask a new contact for an appointment on short notice.

Now let's examine how to follow up after an original appointment postpones:

If the appointment postpones (the fish wants to run), let them go, but don't let the "line go slack." What I mean by that is call or text or email again to follow up about a week after the postponement or your last attempt to call. The same day and time, a week later, is about the best time for first follow-up in my opinion. It's not too soon to appear desperate (which is similar to jerking the line if we use the fishing analogy again). But it's also not too long to appear unprofessional, as if you forgot. (Which lets the "line of communication" go slack.)

First follow-up call: 7 days later

"Hi Bob, it's Joe, is this an okay time to talk?" (If you get them on the phone.)

"Yes."

"Great, how is your schedule this week?"

"Better than last week!"

… proceed to reset the appointment.

Or, if leaving a message or text: "Hi Bob, you asked me to follow up with you. How is your schedule this week?"

If you get another postponement, or they put you off again, wait 2 weeks to call them back.

3rd postponement or 3rd put off, wait 3 weeks.

4th postponement or no answer, 4 weeks, etc.

These are just guidelines, mind you. But the point is, you want to keep the relationship warm. Phoning too often can cool off that warm prospect. Not following up professionally can also result in them doing business with someone else because they lost your number or thought you forgot about them.

An example of a 3rd or 4th call back:

"Hi Bob, I forgot who was supposed to call who back, so I thought I would call. Have I caught you at a bad time?"

"No. It's good. Sorry we haven't called you back. It's been hectic."

"No problem. Are you still interested in getting together to chat?"

"Yes. For sure. It's just this next week is still really busy."

Okay, well, should I give you a call at the end of next week, or would the week after be better?"

"The week after would be better."

"Okay. Chat then. Have a great week."

Now you obviously don't know if they are politely putting you off or not yet. But if they allow you to keep following up, eventually those follow-up calls allow you a few minutes to chat. Over time, the more you chat about what's going on in their busy schedule, the more you **warm up the cool market**.

For example, in the last conversation you could have asked, "Hectic with work?" "New project on the go?" "Kids graduating?" "Are you feeling better today?" etc. The more you find out what is important in their life at the moment, you can ask about it next time you call:

"Hey Bob, Joe here. How's that project going?" "How was your daughter's graduation?" "Is your mom feeling better?" etc. Professional follow-up means you remember what's important to them. If you truly do care about them, they will pick that up. If they do agree to become your client someday, it will likely be because they feel you will take good care of them because of the way you followed up.

If you forget about issues in their life from call to call and just try to set an appointment without taking into consideration what may have caused the lengthy and frequent postponements (especially an illness to a child or themselves or God forbid a death in the family that you forgot about!) you may run rough-shod over their feelings. Which is like trying to "jerk the line" when they are trying to run. They will spit the hook or the line of communication will be broken. You lost them.

So if you don't have a good memory, try to keep short notes of your follow-up calls.

Again, the warmer the relationship, the more likely it is to actually get an appointment.

Here are some other follow-up tips

If you think they are avoiding your number on call display, then try calling from a different number. For instance, while I am waiting for my car to get serviced I'll use the courtesy phone. So now the call display says "Mercedes Benz" or "Jiffy Lube." People will most likely answer a call from Mercedes Benz … But if you don't have a Mercedes yet … oh well.

Maybe make a call from a restaurant, a hotel lobby, or even someone else's house or cell phone.

If they do answer the phone, and sound a little startled that it's you … well, you know you are being avoided. But you can say something like this:

"Hi Bob, it's Joe Smith again. Have I caught you at a bad time?"

If it's "well, yeah, you have …" then say, "I was just waiting for my car to be repaired and thought I would touch base. But I don't want to pester you. Are you still interested in getting together to discuss that tax saving option or not?"

Sometimes a home landline with a different name on it instead of your cell phone, may also work to help you get their attention.

And go from there.

But these are last resorts. If people are trying to avoid you, then avoid them. No sense aggravating the situation. Besides you have a hundred names on your list, right? You are still making your 5 new calls right? Not JUST follow-up calls right?

Well, good then. Who cares about people who don't want to talk to you? There are lots more who do.

So practice the 5 P's of follow-up: **Be Pleasantly and Professionally Persistent with People who Postpone**.

Especially, if they really are worth following up. Nothing wrong with long-term follow-ups with people who are non-committal but remain friendly. Mailing or emailing them an interesting article about the program you are offering once in a while is also a good way to follow up with the right people.

But don't worry about the ones who spit the hook. There's plenty of fish in the sea.

Once you have become proficient at prospecting, setting appointments and following up....

Congratulations! Now *you* are the teacher!

Training and Motivating Others to Set Appointments

The Art of Duplicating Your Skills and Success in Others

I was very blessed to have great mentors in my life. One of the best was Hector LaMarque, a former jewellery store manager who started selling financial services in his late 20s. He built a substantial financial services business and currently earns over $100,000 A MONTH.

I was working very hard trying to build my own business, and doing everything I possibly could to grow and make money. I was good too because I was making lots of personal sales. But I was dismayed that the new reps in my business weren't following my lead. They would come to my training meetings, but day after day, week after week, they just didn't seem to be doing very much.

I was frustrated with them so I called Hector and asked him why they weren't doing anything.

Here is what he said that changed my business:

"Do your people know what they are doing?"

"Well, yah, I guess."

"Barry, **if your people were as good as you are, what would your business look like?"**

"Well, it would look awesome! I am really killing it right now!"

"Well, *if your people are not as good as you are, why aren't they, and what are you going to do about it?"*

It was that question that caused me to actually analyze what I was doing to set appointments and break the process down to teachable and understandable steps.

When I actually broke down the process of setting appointments I was successfully using, it actually took 17 individual steps to arrive at the results I was getting!

Similar to a pro golfer who makes a drive or putt look easy, it takes *practicing* a number of important movements sequentially to make the "swing" look that easy and fluid. **Perfect practice makes perfect.** Prospecting and appointment setting takes a certain amount of hours of practice as well. Fortunately, learning to set appointments shouldn't take nearly as much practice as golf, but may earn you a similar "pro salary."

Once you have the skills down yourself, and start having

success, other salespeople will want to know your secrets. If you are a sales trainer, or leader/manager of a group of sales people, now you can benefit by teaching these skills to others and thereby **compounding your efforts** … which, if you have the right compensation program, will also compound your income way beyond what you can do by yourself. Having more and more of your income coming from a team of people rather than just your self, will give you the freedom and security most only dream of.

And that's exactly what happened to me. Here is how to do it too.

1. Break your training down to the basic fundamentals. Usually setting appointments, doing presentations, closing the sale, recruiting, customer/rep service.

2. Break down each fundamental into bite size, learnable pieces.

    For example: bring your list of names and show how to add to it using a variety of "memory joggers."

3. Have frequent training (daily or every second day if possible but minimum once a week) for no more than 45 minutes to an hour.

4. Introduce the skill. "How to put names on your list." Teach it. Give them homework to accomplish before the next training (i.e., add 25 to 50 names to your list).

5. Review results of homework at next training. Praise the ones who did the work. "Wow, you got 80 new names?! How did you do that?"

6. Pick up the ones who failed, or teach them how to overcome areas of concern. "Try the next technique – *Prospect as you go* to pick up names when dropping kids at school, morning coffee shop, dry cleaners, etc.…

7. Make sure that skill is learned before you move on to introducing and teaching the next skill. It may sound too slow or too minimal of a skill development, but a strong foundation of basic skills can build confident productive reps where only fear and distraction were present before.

8. Move on to the next skill. "Preparing to make calls."
   Make sure they understand the importance of each step.

9. Role play and practice basic scripts, as well as how to choose which one to use.

10. Be patient. Don't expect everyone to get it the first time. Take it one skill at a time. Don't feel you have to get fancy.

11. If your senior people master the skill quickly, get them to help teach parts of the skill to the others who do not get it as quickly.

12. When the majority of your team starts having success, move on to the next fundamental. After Prospecting would be Appointment Setting, Presenting, Closing, etc.

13. It is critical in my view, that the leader/ teacher leads by example and does exactly what you want your reps to do. They may not get great results to talk about initially, so it is very important that you continue to have good results to share with them, to encourage them, and also keep you sharp. When others start having good results, they take over the talking and you can just moderate the meeting.

Coaching Tip

Let's say you are a sales manager or leader and you have a few reps that are experienced, but not doing very many appointments.

At your regular rep training/info meeting, and after they have watched a motivational video, or listened to an empowering training talk, try this:

Leader: "How many appointments would you like to have next week?" (assuming you are leading reps that aren't subject to a quota)

Rep: "Well, 3 or 4."

Leader: "How many contacts does it usually take for you to get one appointment?"

Rep: "Well, about 4 or 5."

Leader: "So If you want to have 3 appointments next week, you would have to make about 15 contacts, is that right?"

Rep: "Yah, I guess so."

Leader: "So, IF you were to contact the first 5 people, who would they be, and when would you contact them?"

Rep: "Well, I would call A, B, C, D, and E and I could probably contact them this evening."

Leader: "If you were to contact A, what would you say?"

(If they say something that sounds reasonably effective, good, if not, coach them and roll play with them.)

Leader: "Okay, great. After you make those five contacts, text me and let me know how it went and we will talk then, okay?"

Rep: "Okay."

Leader: "Review the instructions in chapter 4 of the "Prospecting and Setting Appointments Made Easy" book before you make your contacts though, okay?"

Rep: "Okay!"

Sometimes motivated reps in a slump just need a little push and some clear instructions to get them going again. If they don't make the calls, they aren't self motivated enough. Don't waste any more personal coaching time on them. If they make the calls but get poor results, coach them over the phone as promised. If they still get poor results, they have a credibility issue. Get them to review the sections in chapter 3 on "How to Warm Up the Cool Market" and "How to Get People to Like and Trust You." If they continue to have poor results, suggest they move on to a different career.

Understanding The Sales Process

The Art of Focussing on Results vs. Distractions

"Not a wheel turns, until a sale is made."

– Peter Thomas, founder of Century 21 Canada

When it comes to training others and even moving toward Mastery yourself, it's important to fully understand the Sales Process. If you don't fully understand this process, or don't communicate it effectively to your reps, they, and you, will get bogged down into distractions that don't lead to results. Actually, you will get results. Just poor ones. This chapter will help you to not get "Mired in Mediocrity."

Sales is a much maligned profession. Most people think sales is what you do if you are poorly educated or can't do anything else for a living.

In some cases, that's quite true. But my dad had a mechanical engineering degree from the University of British Columbia and was a highly regarded truck and auto mechanic in the 1950s and '60s, owning a number of gas stations and repair shops in Vancouver.

Because of his renowned mechanical ability, he was offered the opportunity to own a new car franchise dealership. He left mechanics and became the first Mazda dealer in Canada in 1969. I was 9 years old. I proceed to watch as he built a great franchise in the world of "selling" instead of fixing cars.

So I grew up believing that sales was an okay profession.

Since the economy was in recession in the early to mid-1980s, I was often unemployed, so I kept looking for some kind of sales job to tide me over until I could get a "real job."

The interesting thing about sales, is that it is relatively easy to get in and out of if you have to, as I did in between flying jobs. So if you are unemployed, or fear you may be laid off, or can't seem to find a job in your chosen career, then it is handy to have some sales skills to tide you over. You may find you can make more money in sales than you ever thought possible in your chosen career, as I did. At the very least, if you can develop the skills to get others to believe in you and purchase your product or service, you will never be unemployed again.

"Sales is the lowest paid easy work and the highest paid hard work there is."

Most sales people are paid on a commission basis. The problem with sales, of course, is if you don't sell, you don't make money.

If you are in the business of sales and are not making a lot of money, it's often because it's easy to fool yourself into doing activities that won't lead to sales.

By establishing definitions of the sales process, you can at least become more aware of what activities will produce the results you desire and which ones are simply **work avoidance**.

Here are some basic, but critical **Definitions of the Selling Process**:

1. **Your Market** – people who like you and trust you and can benefit from your product or service, or give you referrals.

2. **Client** – a person who happily owns your product or service.

3. **Prospect** – a future client or customer.

4. **Prospecting** – putting names on a list. If you skipped chapter 2 or forgot this already, it bears repeating - Isn't prospecting all about going to malls, networking meetings, job fairs, etc., and striking up conversations with complete strangers? Like, getting their names and numbers and turning them into excited clients, recruits or referrals? No, it's not. See chapter 2.

5. **Appointment** – face-to-face, nose-to-nose, toes-to-toes,

eyeball-to-eyeball, belly-to-belly with someone who can *become a client*. Screen-to-screen via Skype also qualifies as long as you have the ability to get a signature, cheque, or some other kind of financial commitment.

6. **Presenting** – explaining your product or service to a prospective client. *Note*: Your initial presentation should be able to be done in no more than 20 minutes. "Sell the sizzle, not the steak."

7. **Closing** – asking for and getting a cheque, signature or other form of commitment to do business with you.

8. **Work** – being on an appointment, or trying to get one. *Super critical that you really get this one!*

9. **Contact** – face-to-face, text, phone, email, twitter, facebook, or other means that give you the opportunity to ask for an appointment and get a *yes* or a *no*, or even a *not right now*.

10. **The Phone** – used to make a contact for an appointment. NOT to give a presentation.

11. **Making a Phone Call** – punching in the full 10 digits, getting a live person on the other end.

That's it. The Previous 11 definitions are the Definitions of WORK in the Sales business. If you work hard on those 11 things, you will make money. Everything else is NOT WORK.

The more you spend time not working, the less money you will make. Period.

Here are the areas of chronic NON-WORK or work avoidance that ruin most salespersons careers:

1. **Research**

    "I have to know more about my product before I can sell it."

    Wrong. Assuming you have basic product training, don't overdo it. Often the more you know, the less you sell.

    "Don't drown your prospects in your fountain of knowledge."

2. **Writing emails or follow-up phone calls to potential clients that never commit**

    "But they say they'll do business soon, I just need to stay in touch!"

    Just because it's easier to do "follow-up" calls instead of making calls to new prospects doesn't mean pestering your "follow-ups" every other day. It makes you look desperate and not busy enough. You will eventually turn those prospects off if you don't mix a healthy number of new prospect calls and appointments in with your follow-up calls.

3. **Attending training seminars**

    "These help me learn how to sell!" I believe in attending all training sessions. But just remember, it's not work. It's an activity that you invest your time in only if it motivates or empowers you to produce *immediate* work-related sales activity (i.e., an appointment or a sale within 24 to 72 hours after "training"). If that doesn't happen, then you are fooling yourself and wasting your time and money. *Note to Trainers: if your training meetings do not generate "immediate" results from your trainees, you have the wrong trainees or your "training" is ineffective. See chapter 7.*

4. **Doing Paperwork**

Yes, I know, the job isn't done until the paperwork is complete. But the time to do your paperwork is late at night after you have done all your appointments. (Yes, I know you're tired, but get it done anyway.) Otherwise you will end up having to do it in the middle of your work day when you should be working. (See definition of work.) Or get your paperwork done first thing in the morning before your appointments if you are a morning person.

5. **Going Prospecting**

"What did you do all day"?

"I was prospecting."

"Did you set any appointments, or give any presentations?"

"No, but I got some great leads!"

"How many?"

"Uh, well, I talked to this one guy who asked for my card and said he would give me a call ...."

If I had an annoying-sounding buzzer to push right now I'd press it REAL HARD!! FAIL!

Notice that Prospecting doesn't fall into the "work" category. Only contacting prospects with an attempt to set an appointment is work. By the way, I have never in all my 25 years had someone call me off my business card. It's just ID. Or a replacement for a toothpick.

Besides, if you truly master chapter 2, Prospecting won't take "all day."

This is not an exhaustive list... actually it is. I'm exhausted just thinking of all the excuses I've made, or other reps have made to me over the years. Let's just get to **work**, shall we?

Social Media, Do-Not-Call Lists and Call Display

Warning: *Before you make any calls to a cool or warm market or sometimes even a hot market list, check the national* Do-Not-Call List *before you do.*

I never cold called but I know several people who have, and some actually had good success with it. However, cold calling can also ruin a market by annoying people.

Since the introduction of Privacy Laws and Do-Not-Call lists, this practice has largely gone away, which I believe is a very good thing.

However, the Do-Not-Call List does create somewhat of a

barrier to setting appointments with people if, again, your business depends on one-to-one contact.

That's why I believe that it is even more important to master "Warming Up the Cool Market" method of putting names on a list. In essence, having some kind of basic personal relationship and permission to call, is what allows you to bypass the Do-Not-Call list problem altogether. However, if in doubt, check your DNC list, before you make your calls just to be sure.

Using social media is certainly a method of putting names on a list. The younger you are, chances are the more effective your use of Facebook, LinkedIn, Twitter, Instagram, etc. and the more you may be able to get appointments with these methods. The older you are, likely the less you have "grown up" using these tools and the more awkward or difficult they may be for you to use. This compounds your anxiety if you feel you have to use social media to grow your business.

However, my observation of social media after listening to other salespeople and attending social media work shops, is that the desired effect of bringing in more leads is somewhat limited and not as effective as most think. Furthermore, even if you are successful at getting a response from a potential buyer, you still have to cultivate a one-on-one relationship.

The vast majority of great client relationships come from exactly that: a great relationship.

Although relationships can be *initiated* through social media, they are *developed* through regular communication. If social media helps you develop new relationships to the point where you can ask for appointments or an opportunity to present your offering, then more power to you.

However, **the most valued levels of client development communication** in my opinion, are, in this order:

#1.   Face-to-face

#2.   Voice-to-voice

#3.   Text-to-text

#4.   Email-to-Email

#5.   Facebook-to-Facebook

#6.   Website

Numbers 3 to 6 can work to warm up the cold and cool market, but you normally need 1 and 2 to close a transaction.

Therefore, if you develop the skills to get in face-to-face or voice-to-voice contact, you will shorten the route to client development. In other words, you will develop clients quicker and more effectively through the phone and in person.

Social media casts a wide net. But you can get your net tangled in "other fishermen's nets." Or you can be fishing in crowded waters. (Increased competition.)

So if we go back to the fishing analogy for a minute, **concentrate on catching one at a time, before you go after the masses**.

Because I became very good at prospecting and setting appointments one on one, I had more than enough personal activity to keep me busy making money. Also because I mastered this fundamental, I was able to teach it effectively to others who were able to add and multiply my volume. Some got good at other methods of creating leads, like booths in trade fairs, chamber of commerce networking sessions, and social media interactions, among others. But they all still have to convert those leads to face-to-face appointments and one-at-a-time sales.

"But, Barry, I need more volume!"

Okay, do it your way then. While you are spending your time and money investigating social media and following up random cold leads, I'll be making my 5 calls every two days, and warming up the cool market. By the end of 90 days, I'll be kicking your butt.

Why?

Because one-on-one happy client development, and referrals from them to more happy clients, depend on the strength of RELATIONSHIPS.

Building strong relationships takes time. If you are too busy following up random mass marketed leads, you miss the opportunity to develop relationships with people who actually LIKE you.

I am not saying don't have a social media presence. But the core strength of most salespeople's business income will be built on a maximum of about 100 relationships. And about 20% of those are close relationships that drive the majority of your business volume. I would be surprised if you have strong client relationships with more than 50 people.

The volume you need to get your business off the ground or to take it to another level is generated by the upfront consistent habit of contacting people for appointments. The volume of contacts you make that lead to appointments and sales, creates your *"number" – your ratio of appointments to successful client development.*

ANY OTHER ACTIVITY THAT DISTRACTS FROM THAT IS WASTED TIME AND EFFORT.

Maybe not totally wasted, but unless you have lots of time and money to blow, stick to the definition of work previously mentioned: "Being on an appointment or trying to get one." And do not fool yourself. Because if you do, people who work my method will pass you like you are standing still. I have seen it hundreds of times.

But you may argue, "Well, if I am working my Facebook leads and Twitter leads and LinkedIn leads to get an appointment, that IS work according to YOUR definition!"

Fine. Here is the litmus test: if your Facebook, Tweets and LinkedIn conversations involve you ASKING FOR AN APPOINTMENT AND THEM REPLYING YES, NO, OR NOT RIGHT NOW, you can count that as a successful attempt.

If the conversation does not include that, IT'S NOT WORK!

"But, Barry, I am warming up the cool market! Like you said!"

Good for you. But it's still not work. It's prospecting. Remember? If you have names on your list, call them first. If you have no names on your list, social media marketing is ONE method of getting names on your list to try to make appointments with. But it's not the only one.

Some of you will be happy to hear this because you are anxious about not being knowledgeable about social media and need the confidence to continue "the old fashioned way." Some of you who were looking for tips to be more effective in social media marketing may be choked when you hear this but I am going to re-state it anyway: If social media marketing doesn't result in qualified face-to-face appointments fairly quickly, then it is a DISTRACTION FROM WORK.

Sorry to be so tough on you. My intention is to be tough on keeping the focus on activity that makes money. I have seen too many great people run out of money because they spend too much time on the wrong things. Then they get discouraged and quit because the people who they spent all this time "networking" with did business with someone else or weren't interested in the first place.

My point is, if your "prospecting" attempts do not lead to you asking for, and getting appointments in a reasonable period of time, you never really know if you have a potential client or not. If the person is not interested, you should know fairly quickly so you can move on to someone who is.

Having said that, here are a few tips from people who use social media effectively in my opinion. Hope these help.

Facebook – good for keeping track of your clients and friends' life changes that may require your services. But again using Facebook to prospect without developing those friendships can cool your market off.

LinkedIn – valuable for people searching for you to verify your credentials.

Personal Website – valuable for people googling you or looking for services like yours in their geographical area.

Twitter – unless you are a guru of knowledge in your field, I have yet to see the value of having a regular presence on Twitter.

I personally find these methods more of a pest than a help. But I'm in my 50's. Lol. And I don't have to prospect or sell anything anymore to make a living. But, even today, I still use the basic skills outlined in this book, to lobby government on important issues, develop new friendships, help my children find jobs, and advance other projects for myself, my family and friends.

Call Display. I believe in Call Display. I prefer seeing a person or company name on my call display versus "unknown number". I may choose to answer or not. If they leave a brief, polite message, that further identifies who they are and why they are calling, I may return the call, or, answer the next time they call because I am aware of what they want. I may say sorry not interested or be quite willing to listen. Either way, if people want to avoid you they'll avoid you. That's why you have lots of names to call and a list you are constantly adding to. Some people will say yes to an appointment, then postpone it and avoid your phone call if they recognize your number. Eventually, they either tell you to stop calling (rare) or they will pick up because they feel guilty because of your polite, never give up, occasional follow-up phone call.

Call display makes it even more critical to get these prospecting, setting appointments and warming up the cool market, techniques down so when someone actually does answer, you have a much better chance at getting a positive response. Because, in today's busy world, it may be the only chance you get to set an appointment with some prospects.

Applying The Law of Attraction
to Setting Appointments

The Art of Getting the Universe to Work For You
Instead of Against You

On a rather warm, sunny, spring day, I was driving out of a parkade in my Mercedes convertible with the top down. I had a nice suit on and was feeling pretty good about myself and the meeting I had just finished.

As I wound slowly down the circular exit ramp inside the parkade I cruised by a couple of young boys probably in their late teens dressed very 'grunge' looking.

I have to admit I was a little nervous driving past them because they seemed as if they were looking for trouble.

As I slowly passed them one of the boys growled, **"I hate rich people."**

Suddenly, it was if a bucket of cold water had been tossed all over the warm, feel-good emotions I was having about myself. I felt deflated, even ashamed and humiliated by that random piece of vitriol from a complete stranger.

What kind of person had I become?! Was I now a pompous, out of touch, entitlement mentality, nasty, rich person that everyone else looked at with scorn?

Had I spent too much money on a car, on my suit, on my haircut?! For god sake! What had I become?

And then suddenly my attitude changed.

Wait a minute.

I used to be that 19-year-old guy standing in the parkade with his buddy, feeling lost, out of touch with the world … angry and not even knowing why.

But, I went to college. Then tried desperately to get a job in my chosen profession and yet was continually frustrated by roadblocks and obstacles beyond my control. Those roadblocks forced me to try an opportunity that was a real gamble, a real risk. But I persevered. I learned the skills it took to make money with my own brain and my own two hands. So no one could lay me off or fire me again. I worked 10-hour days, 6 days a week, sacrificed tremendously, and built a business from scratch with no bank loans or start-up capital that today generates millions of dollars in revenue, taxes, and opportunity for thousands of people. Many of those people never would have had that opportunity if it wasn't for my guts and my positive attitude!

Suddenly, it was that hard-fought-for mental toughness that filled my deflated spirit and gave me the winner's response to that young man's misguided anger.

In the 10 seconds it took for me to think those thoughts and drive down the spiral exit ramp to the opposite side (where there was some distance between me and them, luckily), I heard myself respond to his jeer, "I hate rich people" with:

"Well, I guess you'll never be one then."

The fact that I rebuked him raised his anger to the boiling point. I'm sure if he could have, he would have jumped in my open convertible and hammered me. But thankfully he was too far away. He had to settle for uttering as many expletives as he could think of until he yelled his final threat – "ONE OF THESE DAYS I'LL BE RICHER THAN YOU!"

I could see his face was red, his chest and arms heaving with defiance ... and then his face suddenly changed into the realization that he had just declared he would become exactly what he had just told me he hated! He actually looked a little bewildered as I glanced back at him with a smile, before I drove out of sight.

I think about that young man from time to time, and hope that he actually is "richer than me" today. Maybe I will read an article about him in a magazine where he attributes his multi-million dollar success to an early turning point in his life. When, 20 years ago, as an angry young man standing in a parkade in downtown Victoria, he was skillfully rebuked by an older guy in a convertible Mercedes ....

Moral of the story, if you want to be rich, don't disdain those that are. Or worse, don't consciously wish for good finances while unconsciously thinking that money will bring you problems. Or that you prefer the broke, simple life:

- "Money is the root of all evil."
- "Rich people have to step on poor people to get rich."
- "You change into a nasty person when you get rich."

All of that is crap by the way. But it is what a lot of broke people say. What I say to them if they truly are afraid that money will change them into something they don't like, is:

"Why don't you get rich. If you don't like it you can always be broke again."

You have to align your conscious and subconscious thoughts, similar to realigning the polarity of batteries to provide current. Misaligned batteries have power but can't conduct current. Same as your mind. Make sure you truly align your mental batteries.

For instance, you want money, you want appointments, but secretly you are afraid that you will make a fool of yourself on the appointment. So even if you get up the guts to make a call, the results will often be less than favourable.

"Sorry, Barry, I'm too busy right now."

"Oh good, I didn't really want to go out on an appointment anyway."

Start by *feeling* how good it will be for your prospective client to lean forward and totally be enthralled with your presentation. See them warm up and tell you that this is exactly what they have been looking for and how grateful they are that you showed it to them. Then see them smiling at each other excitedly talking about the three other couples who need to see the same thing!

Now don't you *feel* better about making that call? Practice that technique every time you feel nervous or doubtful. Practice builds the mental strength to hold positive thoughts and keep fear from creeping back in.

Yes, fear can still creep back in. But your mind can really only hold one thought at a time, so why make it a negative one? Why inject FEAR into a phone call you haven't even made yet?!

False

Evidence

Appearing

Real

If you're going to make up false evidence, why not make happy thoughts instead of unhappy ones? Lol.

Happy feelings attract happy people and happy circumstances. Negative feelings attract negative people and negative circumstances.

Sorry. That's the Law. The Law of Attraction.

The good news is 16 seconds of concentrated, focussed, positive imaging and feeling can erase hours of negative energy. For more on this check out Dr. Robert Anthony's *"Power of Deliberate Creation"*, a book and CD series. His 11-minute "Rapid Manifestation" audio has worked more consistently and effectively over a longer period of time for me than any other self-help book or audio series I have ever used.

The only caveat to this series is you have to be in a fairly "up beat" state of mind.

If you are in a down, depressed, anxious, or fearful state of mind you may not be able to benefit from this advanced training.

If you are ever in that down of a mood, try Lynn Grabhorn's bestselling *"Excuse Me, Your Life Is Waiting."* That should get your butt out of a rut and prepare you for Dr. Anthony's teachings.

If that doesn't work, and you are chronically feeling lower than a snake's belly in a wagon wheel rut, *then get professional help*. A "check-up from the neck-up", if you will. Psychologists and counsellors have special training to sort out the root cause of your emotional or mental stress and get you back into a positive, healthy mental and emotional state. Yes, this costs money. Good psychologists can cost $170+ hour. But if they are good, you will only need 3 to 5 sessions with them. If you don't believe it is worth it, or you think you can fix yourself, go ahead. But think of how much your state of mind is slowing you down right now. Think of how much that costs in personal productivity. If your storehouse of emotional and mental strength is almost empty, you have very little to give to others who may need you. If you are a leader, a manager, a parent, you owe it to the people in your care to be strong and on your game. If you absolutely cannot get out of a rut, if your mental state is in chronic "dis - ease", you are costing yourself a lot more than the price of a psychologist. You can NOT afford NOT to get professional help. At the very least, see a counsellor for $65 an hour.

Final definition

Financial Independence – having enough monthly "passive" income coming in from your business or other investments so you can work if you want to, not because you have to.

"Until you are financially independent, setting and doing

appointments is kind of like wrestling with a gorilla. You don't stop when you are tired. You stop when the gorilla is tired."

Here's an inspirational rap poem I wrote and rehearsed with my kids. We really enjoyed practising together and then performing alternating parts in front of an iPhone camera. I believe the repetition helped them absorb the poem's message, and have more confidence and commitment in life – the "right stuff".

You are welcome to do your best rap performances with your sales associates, families and friends. And when your video goes viral, remember that I get a writer's credit, okay? Lol

You Got the Right Stuff!

Ever wonder how some people get Rich?
Why others are broke and some just Bitch?
Ever wonder why some have all the Luck?
While other people's life just seem to Suck?

If you been blamin' your life on distraction,
It's cuz you don't get the law of attraction
Negative thoughts create negative action
That's why you can't get no satisfaction.

You are, and you will be bound
To be like those you hang around
Stay close to where winners are found
Or losin' will chase you round and round.

If you wanna change things up
You're gonna have to suck it up
Grow Up And Get Tough
Cuz things are gonna get rough
When you think you've had enough
It's time to see you got the right stuff.

We can coach you and train you
Try to wash your brain for you
Erase your negativity,
Teach some responsibility
But lack of activity,
And accountability
Will turn you into a liability
To your friends, your family,
Yourself, and everyone else.

It's a crime to say you don't have enuf time
It's not funny, never havin' 'nuf money
Always frustrated and under stress
Maybe it's time to suck it up, Princess!

Don't give me those puppy dog eyes
Stop tellin' yourself those rational lies
You gonna work for the dreams of some other guy?
Or you gonna achieve YOURS before you die?

You can dream of Success And Fame
But if you live in a world of Excuses and Blame
Constantly Playing that Victim Game
It's a shame, but your life's just gonna stay the same.

It's hard to be strong when your mind is weak
Especially to some you'll sound like a geek
But just smile, and turn the other cheek
Knowin' that's what it takes to reach the peak—

Of success,
The pursuit of happiness,
Set apart from the rest,
Bein' the Best of the Best
Laughin' at all the rest ... of the—

The Internet Investigators,
The no-guts Excuse makers
Time-wasting Troublemakers
The next time Procrastinators.

They all quit too soon, took too long,
Said everything was all wrong
And you wouldn't last very long
But you'll prove them all wrong.

It ain't always nice
But get some good advice
You can live without strife
Really enjoyin' your life,

Doin' whatever you please
Avoidin' the negativities
like the disease
that they is
to the biz
and to kidz and your life and happyniz.

So if you want things to shape up
You're Gonna have to Wake Up
And decide to Grow Up,
And Get Tough.
Cuz when the going Stops getting rough,
When you've reached the top,
And you HAVE ENOUGH,
Look in the mirror one day and say:
Dude! You Got the Right Stuff!!

Personality-Driven Success and Failure

The Art of Being an Introvert
in an Extroverted Business

In high school, when I used to sit around with a group of friends listening to their back and forth chatter, I was never very good at jumping in and contributing to the conversation. After sitting listening for what seemed like half an hour, and waiting for the right inspiration, and waiting for the right opening to jump in, and waiting for the talkative ones to take a breath, I would finally seize my chance and utter my contributory opinion, joke, or "cool" off-hand comment. Then ... silence. The group paused momentarily as if I'd said something really dumb or irrelevant.

Then they would just continue talking as if they hadn't heard anything I had said. It was like I wasn't even there.

It was kind of humiliating. So I would just sit there listening and not saying anything to avoid embarrassment. I wasn't sure if my friends were just rude, or they honestly thought I was a nice guy but wasn't worth listening to. As Abraham Lincoln remarked: *"It is better to remain silent and be thought a fool than to speak out and remove all doubt."*

I carried that opinion of myself right through my mid-20's which left me feeling outside the general conversation in many social, educational, or business meeting situations.

Then I became successful in my financial career and suddenly started to get asked to speak in front of groups. Oh great, I thought.

The first time I had to give a talk, I was terrible. I spoke so fast, I could barely understand what I was saying. When the MC got up after I had spoken, I could sense he was "covering" for me because I had obviously said something that wasn't understood or was irrelevant, or perhaps just plain awkward.

But I thought, so what, this business isn't about speaking in front of people, it's about engaging people one-on-one and getting them happily involved in my products and services. Which I had become increasingly good enough at that I got asked to speak again! Oh brother! Not again!

So, to try to avoid the awkwardness of the last time I spoke, I bought a book entitled *"How To Get Your Point Across In 30 Seconds Or Less"* by Milo O. Frank. I read it, prepared my talk around those points, practiced it, and delivered it the next day.

And .... I blew everyone's mind! I actually received loud, appreciative, applause instead of the muted, awkward clapping I received the previous time I spoke. Cool. I could get used to this. And I did. In the last 25 years, I have given talks to thousands of people. If only my high school and college chums could see me now!

My point is this: Even though I was in a "people" business, I was an introvert and didn't know it.

In fact, it was only just recently after reading a great book called *"Quiet"* by Susan Cain, that I fully understood my introverted personality trait.

Essentially, Susan Cain observes that the world is often dominated by extroverts who get their ideas heard and implemented because they are often the loudest, or most motivational personalities in the room. Although, statistically, introverts represent 30 to 50% of any group.

She goes on to say that often ideas, methods and strategies from introverts are ignored because they sound boring or not as exciting as the ideas from extroverts.

But, she continues, if introverts are allowed to continue with their methods and in fact are recognized and rewarded for their quieter, but generally more consistent long term results, it will improve the quality of any organization regardless of their endeavour.

I have to agree with that especially in the world of sales. Early in my career most of the ideas on how to prospect, sell and lead, came from listening to extroverts expounding the virtue and bravery, and excitement, and success of their methods from the stage in front of cheering audiences.

I was motivated, but often couldn't bring myself to use their methods. So I developed my own methods, and over time got more consistent long-term results than some of my extroverted peers. When my production numbers became more noticeable, I started being asked to speak. Often the people that had spoke at the last event were not on the speaking program the next time, because their results and successes were inconsistent.

Another study from Susan Cain's book showed a difference between extroverted and introverted sales managers. Extroverted managers got their sales group selling more volume faster. The introverted sales managers' group started selling a little slower but eventually surpassed the extrovert-led group over time because they had developed more of a cooperative approach instead of one that depended primarily on the motivational abilities of their extroverted leader.

Which is essentially why my sales group eventually surpassed many of my extroverted counterparts who had started before me. I was a teacher, not a preacher, as are most introverts. Everyone loves a good preacher, but without a good teacher to complement the preaching, an organization with 40%+ introverts won't fully develop or sustain long term growth, if it's just about the preaching and motivation. People can get results strictly from being motivated, but *they will get better results if they are motivated AND know what they are doing.*

Here is a tip for introverted sales managers: You have extroverts in your group too. They need preaching, not just teaching.

Get them in front of preachers or motivational videos to supplement your teaching.

As I said earlier, extroverted personalities often don't prepare, they just jump in because they are already motivated and don't have a lot of fear of failure.

That attitude, mind you, is essential in entrepreneurial ventures of any type. I could not have had the success I have had without recruiting extrovert type personalities. They are the spark plugs of the engine. But you still need the pistons to translate energy to productive force. Introverts are the pistons, in my opinion.

Introverts often need a "kick-start" from excited extroverts to get going, especially making calls. But once they get started they keep going even after the extroverts "poop out" or get distracted.

But if even extroverts fear the phone and shy away from too much rejection at times, the rest of us can be paralyzed by fear of the phone and absolutely hate rejection. Those fears prevent us from taking action even when we are super motivated to help our friends with a product or service.

So if you are an extrovert, congratulations on reading this far! Most extroverts I've known over the years, seem to have thicker skins when it comes to rejection, and just want the quick answers to get out there and make some money! Reading and listening are not their strong suits. Talking and taking action are! So, if you just read the scripts on how to set an appointment and want to jump in and call some people – *Go for it!*

But these techniques, and even this book are really for

introverts. However, extroverted sales managers who want to train and motivate their introverted teammates, should learn to teach these skills in this way or at least give their introverted teammates this book. See how easy that is?

In Closing

I truly hope these tips help you to advance the important issues in your life by learning how to prospect and set appointments with the right people in your world. If you truly believe in what you are selling, then you will change the world you live in, one person at a time.

I end with this well-known parable:

> An old man was walking on a rocky beach in the sunshine, picking up sand dollars stranded above the high tide line and throwing them back in the ocean.
>
> A couple, walking by, said to him, "Wow, there are hundreds of sand dollars that get stranded up here every day – do you honestly think you are going to make a difference by throwing a few back in?"
>
> The man looked up at them with another sand dollar in his hand, threw it into the ocean and replied: "I don't know. But it made a difference to that one."

Go make a difference. One phone call, one appointment at a time. You are more powerful than you think.

Appendix I

A Key Strategy and Common Mistakes We All Make

A Key Strategy

My strategy was to make 5 NEW calls every 2 days. (I made follow up calls as well but usually on Tuesdays and Thursdays. And they did not take the place of making new calls.) I liked Monday, Wednesday and Friday for making calls typically around 5:30–6:00-ish in the evening or in the morning around 9:30–10 am, although the times varied depending on who I was trying to reach and how I was trying to reach them. So just like a disciplined exercise strategy, setting appointments also requires discipline and consistency. At least until you get your business "in shape".

So, try this: Pick 45 names off your list. Even if they are 5 easy follow-up calls, don't worry about that for now. All you are trying to do is develop the discipline, which develops the good habit, which will lead to the winning results you want. Divide them up into the 15 you will call for the first 3 weeks and then divide the 15 into the 5 you will call Monday, Wednesday and Friday.

Make your first 5 calls as per the instructions above, and record your results. Take a break on Tuesday and begin again on Wednesday and continue on Friday.

Just like the endorphins you develop after doing something you know is good for you (disciplined exercise, and healthy eating) the same good feelings will come after you make a full week of calls. Plus you get better at the techniques. They become familiar, and you start to "OWN" the process.

And you will start to get appointments!

They say it takes 21 days to develop a habit, so after your third week of calls, you should start to "crave" Monday Wednesday Friday phone call days.

It will be hard, but, like anything else worth doing, it will get easier with practice.

Incidentally, I have not needed to set appointments to see new clients in over 10 years. But, while writing this book, I wanted to test these strategies again, so I followed my own advice given above. It was hard to fit five contacts into my normally full day – especially when I didn't need or want to do any appointments. Did it work? Well, after the first 30 contacts I made, I got more appointments than I could handle. After the 45th contact and third week of calls I have momentum, and excitement, and sales, and even new associates who want to be trained! A whole new phase of my business life is developing and now I actually am "craving" the Monday, Wednesday, Friday phone call days!

So if you want to truly change your business life in 3 weeks, give this strategy a try. Then email me if you like and let me know how it went for you: *bandruschak@gmail.com*

COMMON MISTAKES WE ALL MAKE

Common Mistake #1:
Talking too much.

Have you ever heard the Biblical story of Samson slaying the Philistines?

"It is said that the mighty Samson slew 1,000 Philistines with the jaw bone of an ass (donkey)."

It is also said that 1,000 sales are killed every day with the exact same weapon. Salespeople are notorious for talking themselves in and out of sales. It's painful to watch actually.

That's why in learning how to set appointments on the phone you have to be brief. The call is not designed to give a presentation. Even if the person asks for more info on the phone or by email, do your best to avoid flapping your gums.

Try to compel the person to want to see you to find out more, not keep you on the phone to avoid seeing you.

For instance:

"Can you tell me more over the phone?"

"I would love to but I have an interesting chart that needs a little explanation. I promise I won't waste your time and the ideas I leave you with will either make money or save you money. And, I will buy the coffee! So, listen, IF we were to get together for 20 minutes would you prefer to meet at a Tim Horton's or a Starbucks?"

Also, the same thing in a presentation. Keep it brief. "Sell the sizzle, not the steak." The purpose of your initial presentation with a potential prospect is *to show them just enough to compel them to want to see you again.* If they express interest in what you have to offer, don't keep talking! Use the "IF" transition to set another appointment to close or do a more formal presentation with the required paperwork to start the client/associate development process.

For example: At some point in your brief initial, "eye opener" presentation you should ask this question:

"Does anything I have shown you so far pique your interest?

"Yes. For sure."

"Well, IF you were to get involved with something like this would anyone else be involved in that decision, like your spouse perhaps?"

"Yes, my wife."

"Ok, what is her name and what does she do for a living?"

"Joanne. She is a nurse."

"So if we were to get together with Joanne, would she prefer during the week or are weekends better?"

"Well, she gets a day off on Mondays."

"Ok, I have this Monday afternoon available. What part of the city do you live in?"

"We live near city hall."

"Ok, so why don't you ask Joanne if 1:30 on Monday at your place works and then text me back?"

"Ok, I will text her on her lunch break."

"Great. If we get together Monday, I will show Joanne the same thing I just showed you, plus I have 3 more ideas that could save you or make you money (etc.). If it still piques your and Joanne's interest, we will go from there. If not, maybe you can point me in the right direction. (Or know someone else that could benefit from these ideas.) Thanks! Let me know if Monday is ok with Joanne."

Common Mistake #2:
Talking about things the prospective client or associate isn't interested in.

This is a subset of #1. You have got a person interested in listening to you but you keep adding new information that you think the prospect needs to hear. Chances are they don't need to hear more – *unless they ask you for more information!* In other words, if they ask you a question, answer it as directly as you can, then ask them back: "Does that answer your question?" If they say no, ask them to clarify then answer it again. After you get a positive response, go back to the IF we were to get together to discuss this further, or IF you were to decide to do this… and close for the next appointment. Or another close for the sale would be: "But before I can recommend (any type of X, Y, Z product or service) I need to ask you a few questions…" and then get on your paperwork to start the closing sequence. Closing the sale is beyond the scope of this book. (Maybe in a future book!)

Common Mistake #3:
Stopping when you have success.

In our business we have a common saying: "That stuff worked so good we stopped using it!" The same thing will happen here. A good appointment setting discipline *will yield results.* So, you will need *extra* discipline to keep setting appointments after you start *doing* appointments. Unless, you are only interested in earning good money *once in a while* and taking lots of time off. I personally wanted to build a business that would continue to grow without me. A generation to generation, wealth creation machine, that benefitted not just my family but the lives of thousands of people. That's why I kept the appointment setting discipline consistent for a longer period of time. But that is your and your family's choice.

If you want to get great long term results, you have to *be your own boss* at night before you go to bed. As your boss, set your agenda for the next morning making sure you schedule the 5 people you are going to call. Then as *your employee* the next day – DO AS YOUR BOSS INSTRUCTED you to do the night before. Don't slack off. Be a good boss and give yourself good instructions to follow the next morning. Be a good employee and FOLLOW YOUR INSTRUCTIONS! What did you think BEING YOUR OWN BOSS actually means?

Common Mistake #4:
Being impatient with people or expecting too much from them too soon.

When you are a trainer, trying to duplicate your skills in others, remember that not everyone gets it that quickly. Take your time teaching the fundamentals. It may become boring especially if you are an "A" type personality. But my goal was to have lots of self-motivated productive people who didn't need me to hold their hand. So I put up with boring training and repetition, to have an exciting life surrounded by competent trainers who were motivated to build their own businesses. If that's what you want then remember this: Be ruthless with YOUR time and Gracious with people. Not the other way around. In other words, stay super focussed on the fundamentals of WORK listed above and dedicate about 20% of your time to the effective training of others. As your income grows to over $100,000 and $200,000 you can dedicate more time to training.

But if you ever want to grow your income past those milestones, again, it's important that you re-establish your appointment setting routine as outlined in this book.

The fundamental rule of leadership is: *Leaders should do what they want their people to do.* Work if you want your people to work. Make money if you want your people to make money.

Save money if you want your people to save money. And so on. Followers don't do what you say. They do what you do.

Common Mistake #5:
Not understanding how luck happens.

All the work it takes to read this book and implement the strategies, and be disciplined to prospect and set appointments day after day, week after week, even if the results are slow, fast, or disappointing.... will pay off. I promise you. Because, as the great motivator and winning coach, Art Williams, always used to say:

"The Harder you work, the Luckier you Get."

So, if you want **Luck** to be on your side, **Work HARD**.

Luck

Do you believe in luck? I should say I do. It's a wonderful force. I have watched the careers of too many lucky people to doubt its efficacy.

You see some person reach out and grab an opportunity that the other person standing around had not realized was there. Having grabbed it, they hang on with a grip that makes the jaws of a bulldog seem like a fairy touch. They call into their play a breath of vision. They see the possibility of the situation, have the ambition to desire it, and the courage to tackle it.

They intensify their strong points, bolster their weak ones, cultivate their personal qualities that cause other people to trust them and co-operate with them. They sew the seeds of sunshine, of good cheer, of optimism, of unstinted kindness. They give freely of what they have, both spiritual and physical things.

They think a little straighter, work a little harder and a little longer; travel on their nerve and enthusiasm; they give such service as their best effort permits. They keep their head cool, their feet warm, their mind busy. They don't worry over trifles.

They plan their work and then stick to it, rain or shine. They talk and act like a winner for they know in time they will be one. And then – LUCK does all the rest.

— Anonymous

Bibliography

The Automatic Millionaire – David Bach

Body for Life – Bill Phillips

Dress for Success – John T. Molloy

Excuse Me, Your Life Is Waiting – Lynn Grabhorn

How to Get People to Like You in 90 Seconds or Less –
  at www.wikiHow.com

How To Get Your Point Across In 30 Seconds Or Less –
  Milo O. Frank

How to Master the Art of Selling – Tom Hopkins

How to Win Friends and Influence People – Dale Carnegie

Power of Deliberate Creation – Dr. Robert Anthony

Quiet – Susan Cain

The Secret – Rhonda Byrne

Serious Money – Nick Murray

The Wealthy Barber – David Chilton

Acknowledgements

I would like to thank Hector LaMarque for his mentorship, friendship and leadership all these years. I would like to thank Glenn Williams who was the first person I asked about writing this book. He immediately thought it was a good idea and referred me to Michelle Chastain whose legal and regulatory guidance and encouragement helped me to believe that this could work. Also thanks to our legal counsel in Toronto, Keir Turner, who read the book and guided and encouraged its development as well. To my brother Scott Andruschak, who was one of the first to read the draft and loved it. And to my former partner Seonaid Renwick whose enthusiastic review of the book was a true inspiration, just as she was in the early stages of my career.

And finally to Joe King for his excellent illustrations and most importantly to Bruce Batchelor for his editing and publishing expertise and patience!

I have had many friends and mentors in my life that have helped me become successful. They would be too numerous to mention, but *thank you all.*

KidSport

Since its inception in British Columbia in 1993, KidSport has been providing grants to families facing financial challenges with the costs of organized sport registration fees. With over 180 community chapters across the country, KidSport helps in excess of 60,000 kids each year to get off the sidelines and into the game. KidSport believes that sport skills are life skills and that the lessons learned on the field of play help children to become better citizens.

For more information, visit:
www.kidsportcanada.ca/british-columbia/

Dedication

I dedicate this book to all the aspiring introverted sales people out there who need some basic skills to provide a living for themselves and their family.

And to the extroverted sales managers who desperately want to help their people succeed. You are the spark plugs that get the world moving.

"Not a wheel turns until a sale is made."

If a car is not sold, there is no work for the service and parts men and women. If a financial plan is not set up, there is no work for a mutual fund manager and her back office support team. If outside sales reps don't call on clients, there is no work for manufacturers, and labourers.

— You are all valued and greatly appreciated.

I also dedicate this book to all the wonderful volunteers at KidSport. Their efforts will improve the lives of an entire generation of youth through sports. I hope that the proceeds of this book will help them increase their valuable work in communities all across the country.

About the Author

Barry Andruschak was born and raised in Vancouver, BC. He has a diploma of Aviation Technology from Selkirk College in Castlegar, BC. After being a charter pilot for 3 years, he was introduced to the A.L. Williams Corporation, now called Primerica Financial Services Ltd., in 1985. He became Primerica Canada's first Regional Vice President independent sales agent in 1986. He currently holds the title of National Sales Director and lives in Victoria, BC with his family.

For personal coaching tips, comments, or bulk book orders, please contact Barry at bandruschak@gmail.com

www.ingramcontent.com/pod-product-compliance
Lightning Source LLC
Chambersburg PA
CBHW050511210326
41521CB00011B/2408